ILLUSTRATED · BY · ALICE · AND · MARTIN

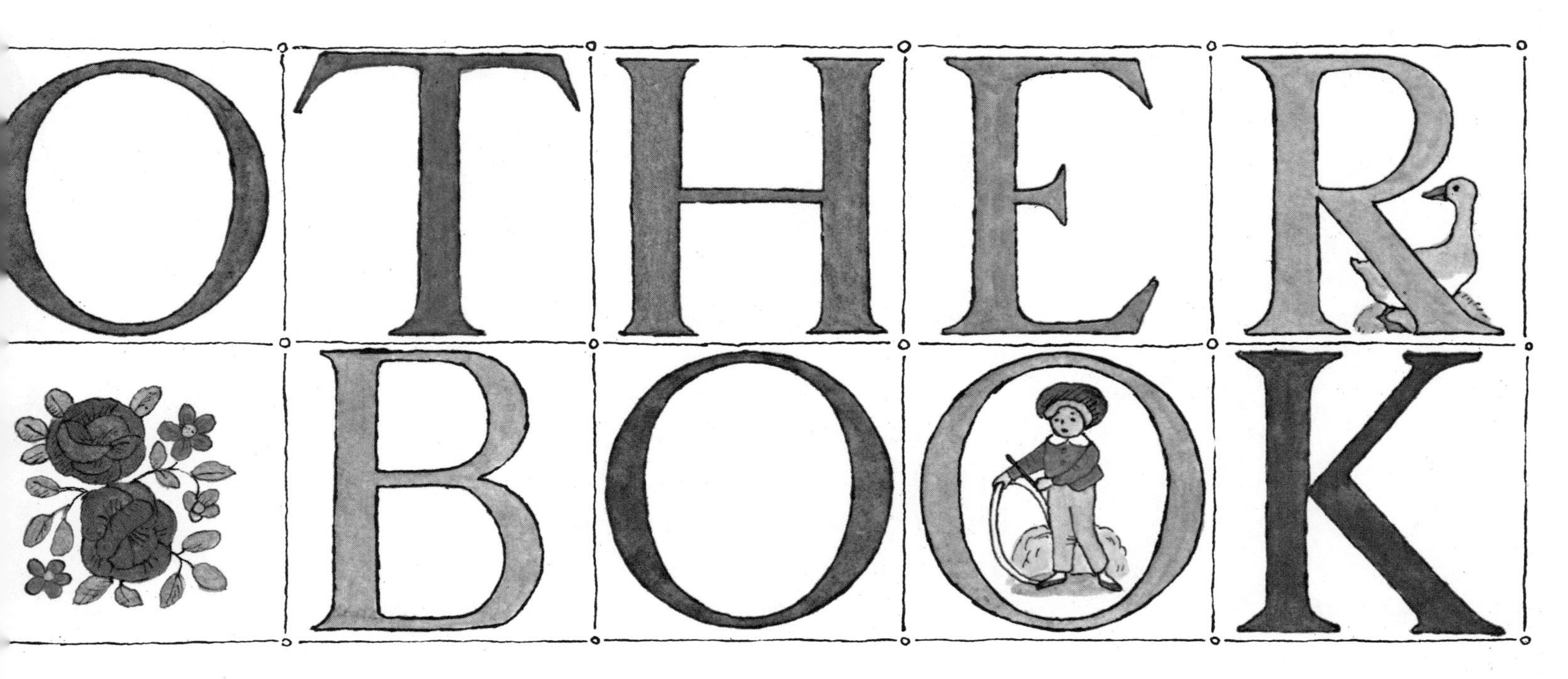


PROVENSEN · RANDOM HOUSE · NEW YORK

Elizabeth, Lizzie, Lisa, and Beth,
They all went together to seek a bird's nest;
They found a bird's nest with five eggs in,
They all took one, and left four in.

 Published in the United States by Random House, Inc., New York, and simultaneously in Canada by Random House of Canada Limited, Toronto.

*Library of Congress Cataloging in Publication Data*

Mother Goose. Mother Goose. Includes index. SUMMARY: A selection of traditional Mother Goose rhymes with illustrations. 1. Nursery rhymes. [1. Nursery rhymes] I. Provensen, Alice. II. Provensen, Martin. PZ8.3M85Prt [398.8] 76-8548 ISBN 0-394-82122-X ISBN 0-394-92122-4 lib. bdg.

Manufactured in the United States of America 10 9 8 7 6 5 4 3

CACKLE, CACKLE, MOTHER GOOSE, have you any feathers loose?
Truly have I, pretty fellow, half enough to fill a pillow.
Here are quills, take one or two, and down to make a bed for you.

Little girl, little girl, where have you been?
Gathering roses to give to the queen.
Little girl, little girl, what gave she you?
She gave me a diamond as big as my shoe.

The cock doth crow
To let you know,
If you be wise,
'Tis time to rise.

The man in the wilderness asked of me,
How many strawberries grew in the sea.
I answered him, as I thought good,
As many as herrings grow in the wood.

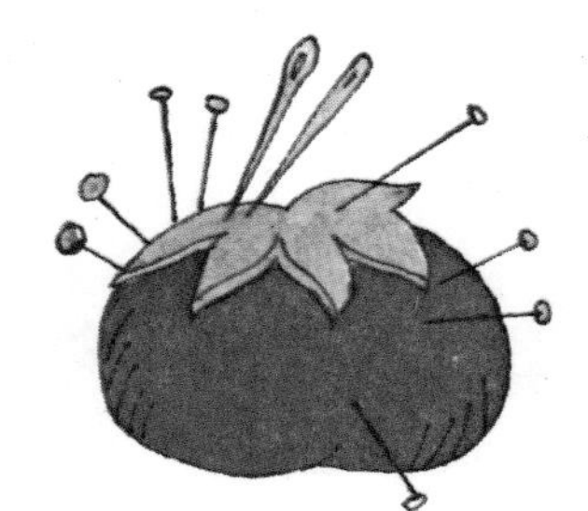

Needles and pins,
Needles and pins,
When a man marries,
His trouble begins.

Little Jack Horner sat in the corner,
Eating a Christmas pie;
He put in his thumb, and pulled out a plum,
And said, What a good boy am I!

Jack be nimble,
Jack be quick,
Jack jump over
The candlestick.

As I was going along, long, long,
A-singing a comical song, song, song,
The lane that I went was long, long, long,
And the song that I sang was a long, long song,
And so I went singing along.

Four stiff-standers,
Four dilly-danders,
Two lookers,
Two crookers,
And a wig-wag.

There were two blackbirds
Sitting on a hill;
The one named Jack,
The other named Jill.
Fly away, Jack! Fly away, Jill!
Come again, Jack! Come again, Jill!

In fir tar is,
In oak none is,
In mud eels are,
In clay none are.
Goats eat ivy.
Mares eat oats.

Goosey, goosey gander,
Whither dost thou wander?
Upstairs, downstairs,
In my lady's chamber.
When the wind is in the NORT
THIRTY DAYS HAT
JANUARY
Brings the snow,
Makes our feet
And fingers glow.
1
WINTER: SLIPPY
Dull NOVEMBER
Brings the blast;
Then the leaves are
Whirling fast.
11
Fresh OCTOBER
Brings the pheasant;
Then to gather nuts
Is pleasant.
10
AUTUMN: WHEEZY, SNEEZY,
A CHERRY YEAR, A MERRY YEAR;
A PEAR YEAR, A DEAR YEAR;
A PLUM YEAR, A DUMB YEAR.
When
the wind
is in the
WEST,
Then 'tis at
the very
best.
Warm SEPTEMBER
Brings the fruit;
Sportsmen then
Begin to shoot.
9
SUMMER: HOPPY, CROPPY, POPPY
8
AUGUST brings
The sheaves of corn;
Then the harvest
Home is borne.
7
Hot JULY brin
Cooling showers,
Apricots,
And gillyflowers.
AS TWENTY-EIGHT DAYS CLEAR AND TWENTY-NINE IN EACH LEAP YEAR
Blow, wind, blow! And go, mill, go!
That the miller may grind his corn;
That the baker may take it and into rolls make it,
And send us some hot in the morn.
When the wind is in the SOUT

e skillful fisher goes not forth.
March winds and April showers
Bring forth May flowers.
EPTEMBER, APRIL, JUNE AND NOVEMBER; ALL THE REST HAVE THIRTY-ONE, EXCEPTING FEBRUARY ALONE, AND THAT
FEBRUARY
Brings the rain,
Thaws the frozen
Lake again.
2
MARCH brings
Breezes, loud and shrill,
To stir the
Dancing daffodil.
3
DRIPPY, NIPPY.
Chill DECEMBER
Brings the sleet,
Blazing fire,
And Christmas treat.
12
EZY.
APRIL brings the
Primrose sweet,
Scatters daisies
At our feet.
4
When
the wind
is in the
EAST,
'Tis neither
good for man
nor beast.
SPRING: SHOWERY, FLOWERY, BOWERY.
MAY brings flocks
Of pretty lambs,
Skipping by
Their fleecy dams.
5
6
JUNE brings
Tulips, lilies, roses,
Fills the children's
Hands with posies.
A swarm of bees in May
Is worth a load of hay;
A swarm of bees in June
Is worth a silver spoon;
A swarm of bees in July
Is not worth a fly.
blows the bait in the fishes' mouth.

Hickory, dickory, dock!
The mouse ran up the clock.
The clock struck one,
The mouse ran down,
Hickory, dickory, dock.

A diller, a dollar,
A ten o'clock scholar!
What makes you come so soon?
You used to come at ten o'clock,
But now you come at noon.

Wee Willie Winkie runs through the town,
Upstairs and downstairs in his nightgown;
Rapping at the window, crying through the lock,
Are the children all in bed, for now it's eight o'clock?

Bell horses, bell horses,
What time of day?
One o'clock, two o'clock,
Off and away!

THE TRAGICAL DEATH OF A, APPLE PIE, WHO WAS CUT IN PIECES AND EATEN
A was an Apple pie
B bit it
C cut it
D dealt it
E eat it
F fought for it
G got it
H had it
I inspected it
J joined for it
K kept it
L longed for it
M mourned for it
A
N nodded at it
O opened it
P peeped in it
Q quartered it
R ran for it
S stole it
T took it
U upset it
V viewed it
W wanted it
XYZ and &
all wished for
a piece in hand

ONE-ERY, TWO-ERY, TICKERY SEVEN; HALLIBO, CRACKIBO, TEN AND ELEVEN.
1, 2,
Buckle my shoe
3, 4,
Shut the door
5, 6,
Pick up sticks
7, 8,
Lay them straight
9, 10,
A big fat hen
11, 12,
Dig and delve
13, 14,
Maids a-courting
15, 16,
Maids in the kitchen
17, 18,
Maids in waiting
19, 20,
My plate's empty.
SPIN, SPAN, MUSKIDAN; TWIDDLE-UM, TWADDLE-UM, TWENTY-ONE.

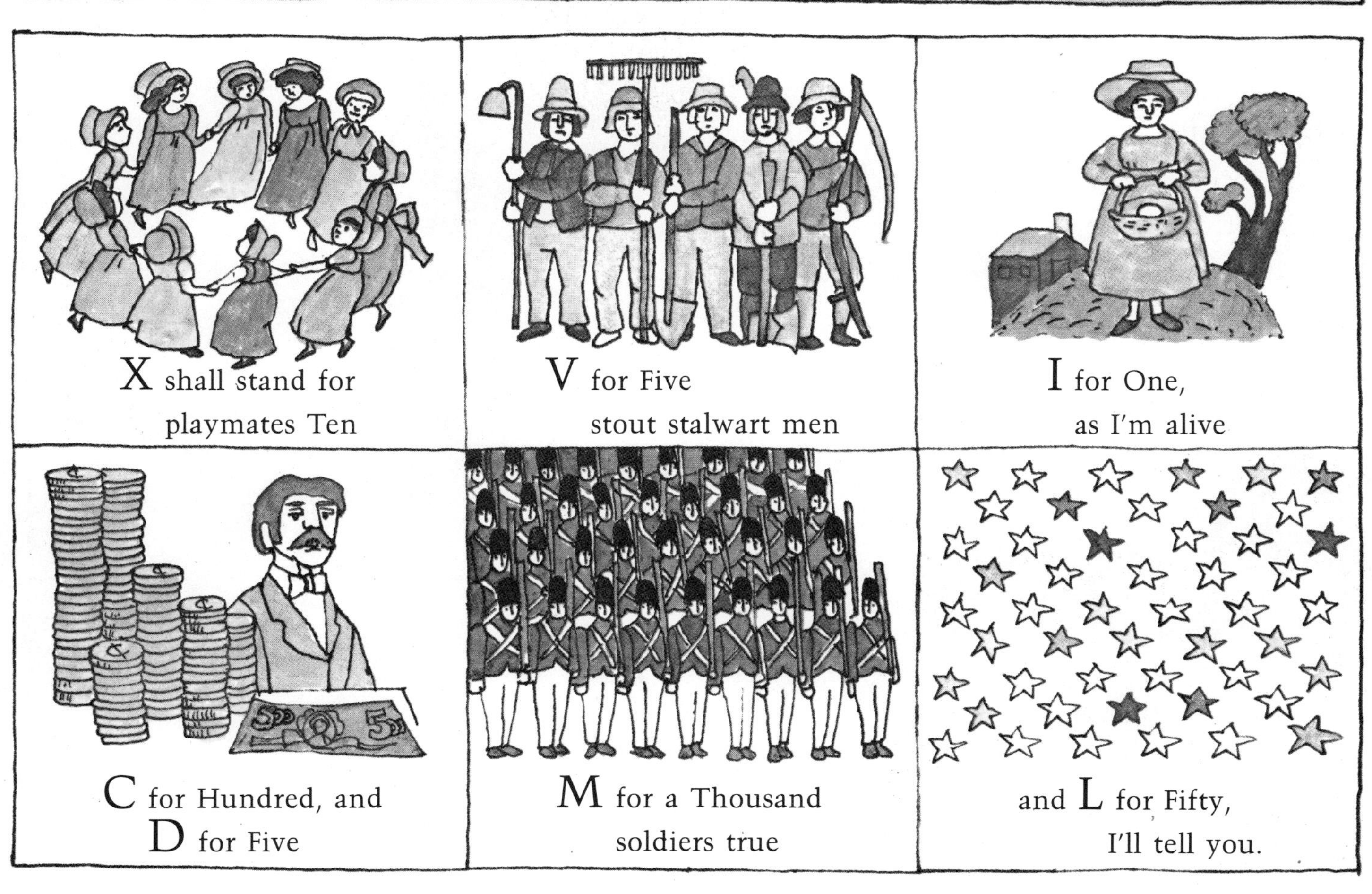
X shall stand for
playmates Ten
V for Five
stout stalwart men
I for One,
as I'm alive
C for Hundred, and
D for Five
M for a Thousand
soldiers true
and L for Fifty,
I'll tell you.

Little Bo-peep has lost her sheep,
And doesn't know where to find them.
Leave them alone,
And they'll come home,
Bringing their tails behind them.

Little Bo-peep fell fast asleep,
And dreamt she heard them bleating.
But when she awoke,
She found it a joke,
For they were still a-fleeting.

Then up she took her little crook,
Determined for to find them.
She found them indeed,
But it made her heart bleed,
For they'd left their tails behind them.

It happened one day, as Bo-peep did stray
Into a meadow hard by,
There she espied
Their tails side by side,
All hung on a tree to dry.

She heaved a sigh, and wiped her eye,
And over the hills went rambling,
And tried what she could,
As a shepherdess should,
To tack again each to its lambkin.

Those dressed in blue have lovers true;
In green and white,
Forsaken quite.

If I am to marry rich,
Let me hear a cock crow.
If I am to marry poor,
Let me hear a hammer blow.

Here am I, little jumping Joan;
When nobody's with me,
I'm always alone.

Baa, baa, black sheep, have you any wool?
Yes, sir, yes, sir, three bags full;
One for my master, and one for my dame,
And one for the little boy who cries in the lane.

The Queen of Hearts
She made some tarts,
All on a summer's day.

The Knave of Hearts
He stole those tarts,
And took them clean away.

The King of Hearts
Called for the tarts,
And beat the knave full sore.

The Knave of Hearts
Brought back the tarts,
And vowed he'd steal no more.

Sing a song of sixpence,
A pocket full of rye;
Four and twenty blackbirds
Baked in a pie.
When the pie was opened,
The birds began to sing;
Was not that a dainty dish
To set before the king?
The king
was in his counting-house,
Counting out his money;
The queen was in the parlor,
Eating bread and honey.
The maid was in the garden,
Hanging out the clothes;
When down came a blackbird
And snipped off her nose.
SIX PENCE DIEU ET MON DROIT
SIX PENCE DIEU ET MON DROIT

There was a little girl who had a little curl
Right in the middle of her forehead;
When she was good she was very, very good,
But when she was bad she was horrid.

This little man lived all alone,
And he was a man of sorrow;
For, if the weather was fair today,
He was sure it would rain tomorrow.

We are all in the dumps,
For diamonds are trumps;
The kittens are gone to St. Paul's.
The babies are bit,
The moon's in a fit,
And the houses are built without walls.

Cross Patch,
Draw the latch,
Sit by the fire and spin;
Take a cup,
And drink it up,
Then call your neighbors in.

Here's Sulky Sue;
What shall we do?
Turn her face to the wall
Till she comes to.

I do not like thee, Doctor Fell.
The reason why I cannot tell,
But this I know, and know full well,
I do not like thee, Doctor Fell.

Little Polly Flinders
Sat among the cinders,
Warming her pretty little toes.
Her mother came and caught her,
And whipped her little daughter
For spoiling her nice new clothes.

Old Toby Sizer is such a miser,
No cloak he'll buy to keep him dry, sir.
He'll not permit his neighbor, Randal,
To light his pipe by his short candle,
For fear, he says, he might convey
A little bit of light away.

# IF WISHES WERE HORSES, BEGGARS WOULD RIDE:

There were three jovial huntsmen,
As I have heard men say,
And they would go a-hunting
Upon St. David's Day.

All day they hunted,
And nothing could they find,
But a ship a-sailing,
A-sailing with the wind.

One said it was a ship,
The other he said, Nay;
The third said it was a house,
With the chimney blown away.

And all the night they hunted,
And nothing could they find,
But the moon a-gliding,
A-gliding with the wind.

One said it was the moon,
The other he said, Nay;
The third said it was a cheese,
And half of it cut away.

This is the way the ladies ride,
Tri, tre, tri, tree, tri, tre, tri, tree!
This is the way the ladies ride,
Tri, tre, tri, tree, tri, tre, tri, tree!

This is the way the gentlemen ride;
Gallop-a-trot! Gallop-a-trot!
This is the way the gentlemen ride;
Gallop-a-trot! Gallop-a-trot!

And all the day they hunted,
And nothing did they find,
But a hedgehog in a bramble bush,
And that they left behind.

And all the night they hunted,
And nothing could they find,
But a hare in a turnip field,
And that they left behind.

And all the day they hunted,
And nothing could they find,
But an owl in a holly tree,
And that they left behind.

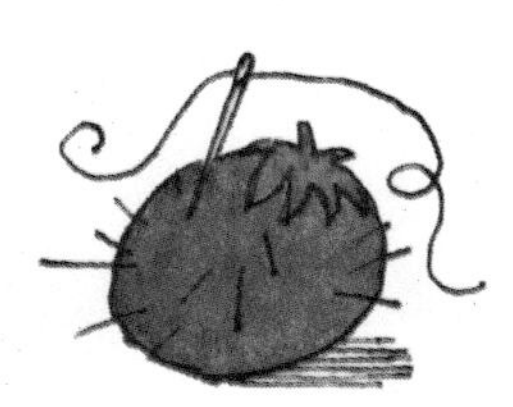

The first said it was a hedgehog,
The second he said, Nay;
The third said it was a pincushion,
And the pins stuck in wrong way.

The first said it was a hare,
The second he said, Nay;
The third said it was a calf,
And the cow had run away.

The first said it was an owl,
The second he said, Nay;
The third said 'twas an old man,
And his beard growing gray.

This is the way the farmers ride!
Hobbledy-hoy, hobbledy-hoy!
This is the way the farmers ride!
Hobbledy-hoy, hobbledy-hoy!

And when they come to a hedge—they jump over!
And when they come to a slippery place—
They scramble, scramble,
Tumble-down Dick!

See-saw, sacradown.
Which is the way to London town?
One foot up and the other foot down,
That is the way to London town.

Leg over leg,
As the dog went to Dover;
When he came to a stile,
Hop, he went over.

Ride a cock-horse to Banbury Cross,
To see a fine lady upon a white horse.
Rings on her fingers and bells on her toes,
She shall have music wherever she goes.

Simple Simon met a pieman, going to the fair;
Says Simple Simon to the pieman, Let me taste your ware.
Says the Pieman to Simple Simon, Show me first your penny.
Says Simple Simon to the pieman, Indeed, I have not any.

Smiling girls, rosy boys,
Come and buy my little toys;
Monkeys made of gingerbread
And sugar horses painted red.

If I'd as much money as I could tell,
I never would cry, Old clothes to sell.
Old clothes to sell! Old clothes to sell!
I never would cry, Old clothes to sell.

If I'd as much money as I could spend,
I never would cry, Old chairs to mend,
Old chairs to mend! Old chairs to mend!
I never would cry, Old chairs to mend.

Pussy cat, pussy cat, where have you been?
I've been to London to look at the queen.
Pussy cat, pussy cat, what did you there?
I frightened a little mouse under her chair.

To market, to market,
To buy a fat pig,
Home again, home again,
Jiggety-jig.

To market, to market,
To buy a fat hog,
Home again, home again,
Jiggety-jog.

Hot cross buns! Hot cross buns!
One a penny, two a penny, hot cross buns.
If you have no daughters, give them to your sons.
One a penny, two a penny, hot cross buns.

Green cheese,
Yellow laces,
Up and down
The market places.

Oh, do you know the muffin man,
The muffin man, the muffin man,
Oh, do you know the muffin man
That lives in Drury Lane?

Barber, barber, shave a pig,
How many hairs will make a wig?
Four and twenty, that's enough.
Give the barber a pinch of snuff.

Cobbler, cobbler, mend my shoe,
Get it done by half-past two.
Stitch it up, and stitch it down,
Then I'll give you half a crown.

Handy Pandy, Jack-a-dandy,
Loves plum cake and sugar candy.
He bought some at the grocer's shop,
And out he came, hop, hop, hop!

There was a maid on Scrabble Hill,
And if not dead, she lives there still.
She grew so tall she reached the sky,
And on the moon hung clothes to dry.

Twinkle, twinkle, little star,
How I wonder what you are!
Up above the world so high,
Like a diamond in the sky.

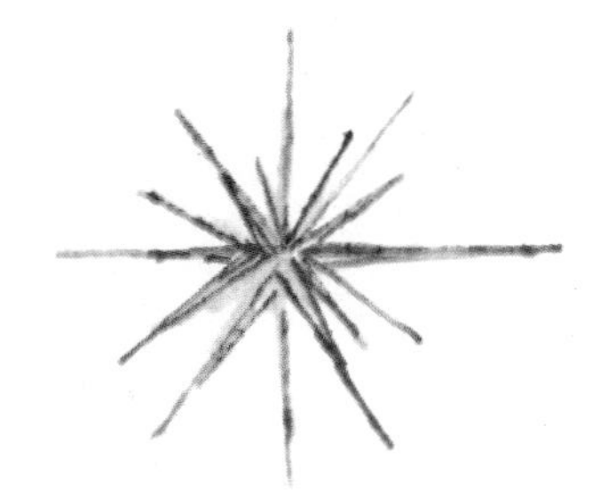

When the blazing sun is gone,
When he nothing shines upon,
Then you show your little light,
Twinkle, twinkle, all the night.

What's the news of the day,
Good neighbor, I pray?
They say the balloon
Is gone up to the moon.

There was an old woman
Lived under a hill,
And if she's not gone
She lives there still.

Jack and Jill went up the hill,
To fetch a pail of water;
Jack fell down and broke his crown,
And Jill came tumbling after.

Old Mother Goose,
When she wanted to wander,
Would ride through the air
On a very fine gander.

Mother Goose had a house,
'Twas built in a wood,
Where an owl at the door
For sentinel stood.

She had a son Jack,
A plain-looking lad,
He was not very good,
Nor yet very bad.

She sent him to market,
A live goose he bought;
See, mother, says he,
I have not been for nought.

Jack's goose and her gander
Grew very fond;
They'd both eat together,
Or swim in the pond.

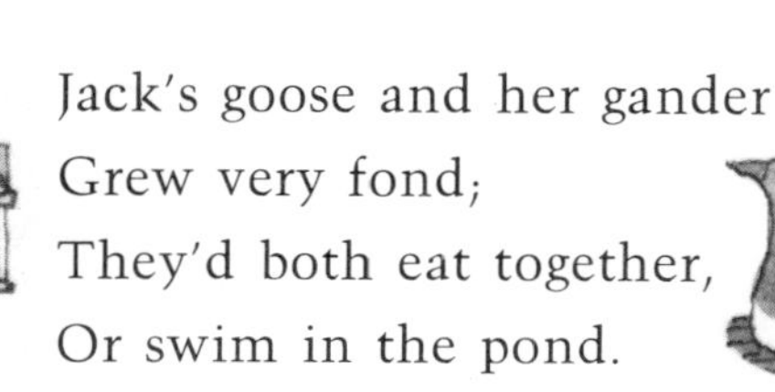

Four and twenty tailors went to kill a snail. The best man among them durst not touch her tail;

Then up Jack got, and home did trot,
As fast as he could caper.

They put him to bed and plastered his head
With vinegar and brown paper.

Jack found one fine morning,
As I have been told,
His goose had laid him
An egg of pure gold.

Jack sold his gold egg
To a merchant untrue,
Who cheated him out of
A half of his due.

The merchant then vowed
The goose he would kill,
Resolving at once
His pockets to fill.

Jack ran to his mother
The news for to tell,
She called him a good boy,
And said it was well.

The gold egg in the sea
Was thrown away then,
But a very odd fish
Brought the egg back again.

Jack's mother came in,
And caught the goose soon,
And mounting its back,
Flew up to the moon.

She put out her horns like a little Kyloe cow. Run, tailors, run, or she'll kill you all e'en now.

A, B, C, tumble-down D,
The cat's in the cupboard
And can't see me.

Jerry Hall, he was so small,
A rat could eat him,
Hat and all.

Upstairs, downstairs, upon my lady's window,
There I saw a cup of sack and a race of ginger,
Apples at the fire and nuts to crack,
A little boy in the cream pot up to his neck.

Peter Piper picked a peck of pickled pepper;
A peck of pickled pepper Peter Piper picked.
If Peter Piper picked a peck of pickled pepper,
Where's the peck of pickled pepper Peter Piper picked?

If ifs and ands
Were pots and pans,
There'd be no need for tinkers' hands.

I had a little husband, no bigger than my thumb;.
I put him in a pint pot and there I bade him drum.
I gave him some garters to garter up his hose,
And a little silk handkerchief to wipe his pretty nose.

Once I saw a little bird
Come hop, hop, hop,
And I cried, Little bird,
Will you stop, stop, stop?

I was going to the window
To say, How do you do?
But he shook his little tail
And away he flew.

A robin and a robin's son
Once went to town to buy a bun.
They couldn't decide on plum or plain,
And so they went back home again.

There were two wrens upon a tree,
Whistle and I'll come to thee;
Another came, and there were three,
Whistle and I'll come to thee;

All of a row,
Bend the bow,
Shot at a pigeon
And killed a crow.

Tweedledum and Tweedledee
Agreed to have a battle,
For Tweedledum said Tweedledee
Had spoiled his nice new rattle.

Just then flew by a monstrous crow,
As big as a tar barrel,
Which frightened both the heroes so
They quite forgot their quarrel.

There was an owl lived in an oak,
Wisky, wasky, weedle;
And every word he ever spoke
Was, Fiddle, faddle, feedle.

A gunner chanced to come that way,
Wisky, wasky, weedle;
Says he, I'll shoot you, silly bird.
Fiddle, faddle, feedle.

Pit, pat, well-a-day,
Little robin flew away.
Where can little robin be?
Gone into the cherry tree.

Another came and there were four,
You needn't whistle any more,

For being frightened, off they flew,
And there are none to show to you.

The north wind doth blow,
And we shall have snow,
And what will poor robin do then?
Poor thing!

He'll sit in a barn,
And keep himself warm,
And hide his head under his wing.
Poor thing!

Magpie, magpie,
Flutter and flee,
Turn up your tail
And good luck come to me.

OLD MOTHER HUBBARD went to the cupboard, to fetch her poor dog a bone;
When she got there the cupboard was bare, and so the poor dog had none.

She went to the baker's
To buy him some bread,
But when she came back
The poor dog was dead.

She went to the fishmonger's
To buy him some fish,
But when she came back
He was licking the dish.

She went to the joiner's
To buy him a coffin,
But when she came back
The poor dog was laughing.

She went to the tailor's
To buy him a coat,
But when she came back
He was riding a goat.

She went to the barber's
To buy him a wig,
But when she came back
He was dancing a jig.

She went to the hatter's
To buy him a hat,
But when she came back
He was feeding the cat.

She went to the grocer's
To buy him some fruit,
But when she came back
He was playing the flute.

She took a clean dish
To get him some tripe,
But when she came back
He was smoking a pipe.

She went to the seamstress
To buy him some linen,
But when she came back
The dog was a-spinning.

She went to the hosier's
To buy him some hose,
But when she came back
He was dressed in his clothes.

She went to the cobbler's
To buy him some shoes,
But when she came back
He was reading the news.

The dame made a curtsy,
The dog made a bow;
The dame said, Your servant,
The dog said, Bow-wow.

they lost their mittens,
And they began to cry,
Oh, mother dear, we sadly fear
Our mittens we have lost.
What! Lost your mittens,
you naughty kittens!
Then you shall have no pie.
Mee-ow, mee-ow, mee-ow.
No, you shall have no pie.

The three little kittens,
they found their mittens,
And they began to cry,
Oh, mother dear, see here, see here,
Our mittens we have found.
What! Found your mittens,
you good little kittens!
Then you shall have some pie.
Purr-r, purr-r, purr-r,
Oh, let us have some pie.

The three little kittens
put on their mittens,
And soon ate up the pie.
Oh, mother dear, we greatly fear
Our mittens we have soiled.
What! Soiled your mittens,
you naughty kittens!
Then they began to sigh.
Mee-ow, mee-ow, mee-ow.
Then they began to sigh.

The three little kittens,
they washed their mittens,
And hung them out to dry.
Oh, mother dear, look here, look here,
Our mittens we have washed.
What! Washed your mittens,
you darling kittens,
But I smell a rat close by.
Hush! Hush!
We smell a rat close by.

RAIN, RAIN, GO AWAY, COME AGAIN ANOTHER DAY.

Doctor Foster went to Gloucester
In a shower of rain;
He stepped in a puddle,
Right up to his middle,
And never went there again.

A sunshiny shower
Won't last half an hour.

One misty, moisty morning, when cloudy was the weather,
I chanced to meet an old man clothed all in leather.
He began to compliment, and I began to grin.
How do you do? And how do you do? And how do you do again?

WHAT ARE LITTLE BOYS MADE OF, MADE OF? WHAT ARE LITTLE BOYS MADE OF?
FROGS AND SNAILS AND PUPPY-DOGS' TAILS; THAT'S WHAT LITTLE BOYS ARE MADE OF.

Charley, Charley,
Stole the barley
Out of the baker's shop.
The baker came out
And gave him a clout,
Which made poor Charley hop.

Little Boy Blue, come blow your horn,
The sheep's in the meadow, the cow's in the corn.
Where is the boy who looks after the sheep?
He's under a haystack, fast asleep.
Will you wake him? No, not I,
For if I do, he's sure to cry.

Diddle, diddle, dumpling, my son John,
Went to bed with his trousers on;
One shoe off, and one shoe on,
Diddle, diddle, dumpling, my son John.

Georgie Porgie, pudding and pie,
Kissed the girls and made them cry;
When the boys came out to play,
Georgie Porgie ran away.

WHAT ARE LITTLE GIRLS MADE OF, MADE OF? WHAT ARE LITTLE GIRLS MADE OF?
SUGAR AND SPICE AND ALL THINGS NICE, THAT'S WHAT LITTLE GIRLS ARE MADE OF.

Little Popple-de-Polly
Said, See my new dolly!
With her beautiful, pop-open eyes.
But I can't make her speak,
Though I've tried for a week;
And whenever I hug her, she cries.

Little Miss Muffet
Sat on a tuffet,
Eating her curds and whey;
Along came a spider,
Who sat down beside her
And frightened Miss Muffet away.

Little Miss Donnet
Wears a huge bonnet,
And hoops half as wide
As the mouth of the Clyde.

Mary, Mary, quite contrary,
How does your garden grow?
With silver bells and cockle shells,
And pretty maids all in a row.

Polly put the kettle on,
Polly put the kettle on,
Polly put the kettle on,
We'll all have tea.

Sukey take it off again,
Sukey take it off again,
Sukey take it off again,
They've all gone away.

Alas! Alas! for Miss Mackay!
Her knives and forks have run away;
And when the cups and spoons are going,
She's sure there is no way of knowing.

An apple pie, when it looks nice,
Would make one long to have a slice;
But if the taste should prove so, too,
I fear one slice would scarcely do.
So to prevent my asking twice,
Pray, Mamma, cut a good large slice.

Pease porridge hot,
Pease porridge cold,
Pease porridge in the pot
Nine days old.

Some like it hot,
Some like it cold,
Some like it in the pot
Nine days old.

Jack Sprat could eat no fat,
His wife could eat no lean,
And so between them both, you see,
They licked the platter clean.

Sippity sup, sippity sup,
Bread and milk from a china cup,
Bread and milk from a bright silver spoon,
Made of a piece of the bright silver moon!
Sippity sup, sippity sup,
Sippity, sippity sup!

The greedy man is he who sits
And bites bits out of plates,
Or else takes up an almanac
And gobbles all the dates.

Little Tommy Tucker
Sings for his supper.
What shall we give him?
White bread and butter.
How shall he cut it
Without e'er a knife?
How will he be married
Without e'er a wife?

Molly, my sister, and I fell out,
And what do you think it was all about?
She loved coffee and I loved tea,
And that was the reason we couldn't agree.

As I was going to St. Ives,
I met a man with seven wives.
Each wife had seven sacks,
Each sack had seven cats,
Each cat had seven kits.
Kits, cats, sacks, and wives,
How many were there going to St. Ives?

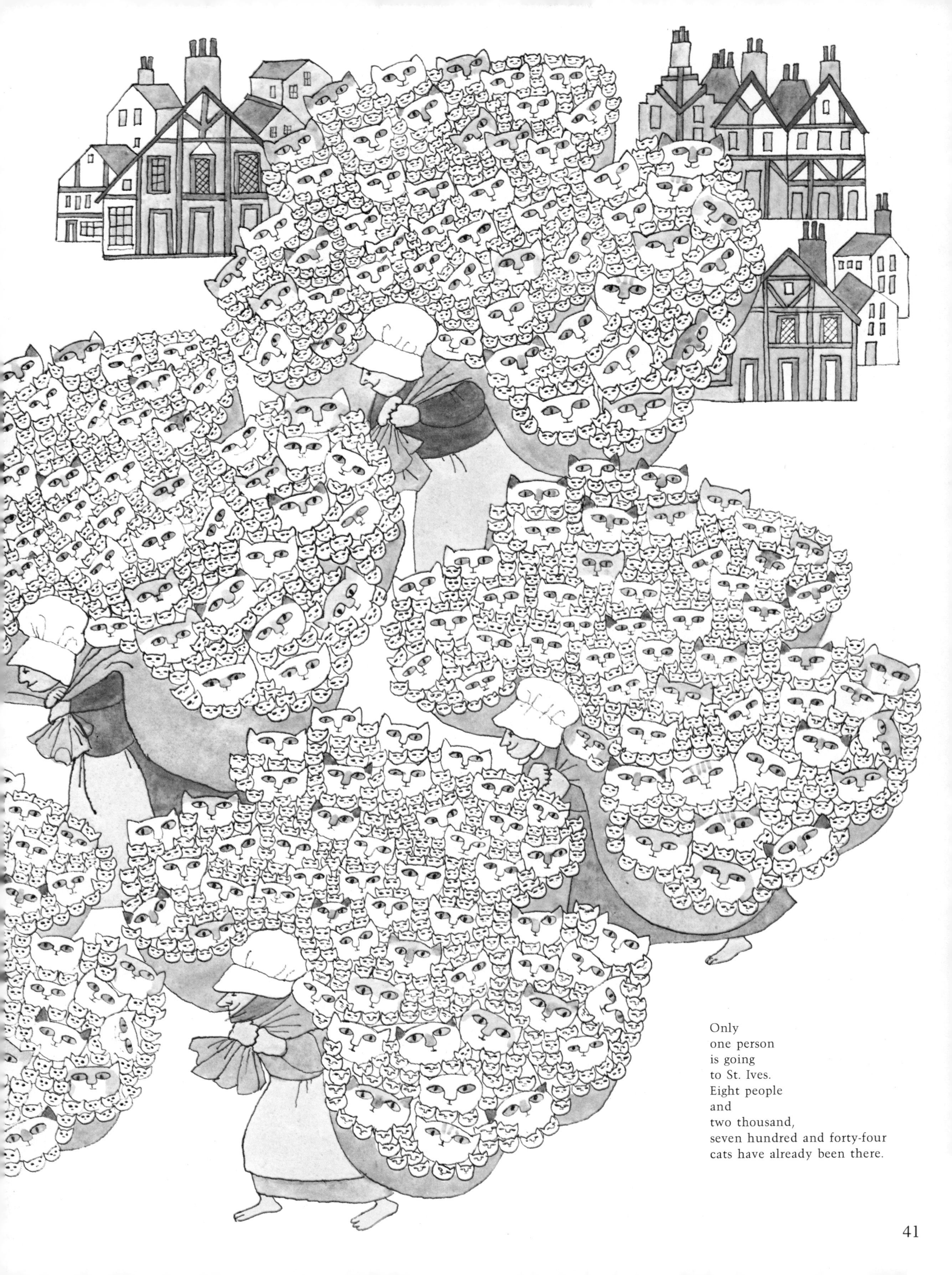

Only
one person
is going
to St. Ives.
Eight people
and
two thousand,
seven hundred and forty-four
cats have already been there.

A little pig found a fifty-pound note
And purchased a hat and a very fine coat,

With trousers and stockings and shoes,
Cravat, and shirt collar, and gold-headed cane.

Then proud as could be, did he march up the lane;
Says he, I shall hear all the news.

## AS I WENT TO BONNER, I MET A PIG

Dickery, dickery, dare,
The pig flew up in the air;
The man in brown
Soon brought him down,
Dickery, dickery, dare.

Tom, Tom, the piper's son,
Stole a pig and away he run.
The pig was eat and Tom was beat,
And Tom went crying down the street.

WITHOUT A WIG, UPON MY WORD OF HONOR.

Elsie Marley
Is grown so fine,
She won't get up to feed the swine,
But lies in bed till eight or nine.
Lazy Elsie Marley.

Tom, Tom, the piper's son,
He learned to play when he was young;
But all the tune that he could play
Was "Over the hills and far away."

This little pig
went to market;

This little pig
stayed at home;

This little pig
had roast beef;

This little pig
had none;

This little pig
cried,
Wee, wee, wee,
all the way
home.

Pat-a-cake, pat-a-cake, baker's man!
Bake me a cake as fast as you can;
Roll it and pat it and mark it with B,
And put it in the oven for baby and me.

Tickly, tickly,
On your knee;
If you laugh
You don't love me.

Brow brinky,
Eye winky,
Chin choppy,
Cheek cherry,
Mouth merry.

I love little pussy,
Her coat is so warm,
And if I don't hurt her
She'll do me no harm.

So I'll not pull her tail,
Nor drive her away,
But pussy and I
Very gently will play.

She shall sit by my side,
And I'll give her some food;
And pussy will love me
Because I am good.

Hush-a-bye, baby, on the tree top,
When the wind blows the cradle will rock;
When the bough breaks the cradle will fall,
Down will come baby, cradle, and all.

Rock-a-bye, baby,
Thy cradle is green,
Father's a nobleman,
Mother's a queen;
And Lizzie's a lady,
And wears a gold ring;
And Johnny's a drummer,
And drums for the king.

Sleep, baby, sleep,
Thy father guards the sheep;
Thy mother shakes the dreamland tree
And from it fall sweet dreams for thee,
Sleep, baby, sleep.

Sleep, baby, sleep,
Our cottage vale is deep;
The little lamb is on the green,
With woolly fleece so soft and clean,
Sleep, baby, sleep.

Sleep, baby, sleep,
Down where the woodbines creep;
Be always like the lamb so mild,
A kind and sweet and gentle child,
Sleep, baby, sleep.

This is the house that Jack built.

This is the malt that lay in the that Jack built.

This is the rat that ate the that lay in the that Jack built.

This is the cat that killed the that ate the that lay in the that Jack built.

This is the dog that worried the that killed the that ate the that lay in the that Jack built.

This is the cow with the crumpled horn, that tossed the that worried the that killed the that ate the that lay in the that Jack built.

This is the maiden all forlorn, that milked the with the crumpled horn, that tossed the that worried the that killed the that ate the that lay in the that Jack built.

This is the man all tattered and torn, that kissed the all forlorn, that milked the with the crumpled horn, that tossed the that worried the that killed the that ate the that lay in the that Jack built.

This is the priest all shaven and shorn, that married the all tattered and torn,

that kissed the all forlorn, that milked the with the crumpled horn,

that tossed the that worried the that killed the that ate the

that lay in the that Jack built.

This is the cock that crowed in the morn,

that waked the all shaven and shorn, that married the all tattered and torn,

that kissed the all forlorn, that milked the with the crumpled horn,

that tossed the that worried the that killed the that ate the

that lay in the that Jack built.

This is the farmer sowing the corn,

that kept the that crowed in the morn, that waked the all shaven and shorn,

that married the all tattered and torn, that kissed the all forlorn,

that milked the with the crumpled horn, that tossed the

that worried the that killed the that ate the

that lay in the that Jack built.

Bow, wow, wow! Whose dog art thou? Little Tommy Tinker's dog, Bow, wow, wow!

BOW-WOW, says the dog;
MEW-MEW, says the cat;
GRUNT-GRUNT, goes the hog;
And SQUEAK, says the rat.
TU-WHU, says the owl;
CAW-CAW, goes the crow;
QUACK-QUACK, goes the duck;
And MOO, says the cow.

See, see! What shall I see? A horse's head where his tail should be.

Wouldn't it be funny? . . . . . . . . Wouldn't it now . . . . . . . .

If the dog said, MOO-OO

And the cow said, BOW-WOW?

If the cat sang and whistled,

And the bird said, MIA-OW?

Wouldn't it be funny? . . . . . . . . Wouldn't it now?

Old Mistress McShuttle
Lived in a coal scuttle,
Along with her dog and her cat.
What they ate I can't tell,
But 'tis known very well
That none of the party was fat.

Peter, Peter, pumpkin eater,
Had a wife and couldn't keep her;
He put her in a pumpkin shell
And there he kept her very well.

Rub-a-dub-dub,
Three men in a tub;
And who do you think they be?
The butcher, the baker,
The candlestick maker;
Turn 'em out, knaves all three!

There was an old woman who lived in a shoe.
She had so many children she didn't know what to do.
She gave them some broth without any bread,
And whipped them all soundly, and sent them to bed.

Hark! Hark! The dogs do bark,
Beggars are coming to town;
Some in rags and some in tags,
And some in velvet gowns.

AS I WAS WALKING IN A FIELD OF WHEAT, I PICKED UP SOMETHING GOOD TO EAT;

Humpty Dumpty sat on a wall,
Humpty Dumpty had a great fall;
All the king's horses and all the king's men
Couldn't put Humpty together again.

NEITHER FISH, FLESH, FOWL, NOR BONE, I KEPT IT TILL IT RAN ALONE.

Hickety, pickety, my black hen,
She lays eggs for gentlemen;
Gentlemen come every day
To see what my black hen doth lay,
Sometimes nine and sometimes ten,
Hickety, pickety, my black hen.

Here we go round the mulberry bush,
The mulberry bush, the mulberry bush,
Here we go round the mulberry bush,
So early in the morning.

This is the way we wash our hands,
Wash our hands, wash our hands,
This is the way we wash our hands,
So early in the morning.

This is the way we wash our clothes,
Wash our clothes, wash our clothes,
This is the way we wash our clothes,
So early in the morning.

This is the way we go to school,
Go to school, go to school,
This is the way we go to school,
So early in the morning.

This is the way we come out of school,
Come out of school, come out of school,
This is the way we come out of school,
So early in the morning.

A ring, a ring o'roses,
A pocket full of posies,
Ashes! Ashes!
We all fall down.

See-saw, Margery Daw,
Jenny shall have a new master;
She shall have but a penny a day,
Because she can't work any faster.

One for the money,
Two for the show,
Three to make ready
And four to go!

London Bridge is falling down,
Falling down, falling down,
London Bridge is falling down,
My fair lady.

Build it up with iron bars,
Iron bars, iron bars,
Build it up with iron bars,
My fair lady.

Here's a prisoner I have got,
I have got, I have got,
Here's a prisoner I have got,
My fair lady.

SEE A PIN AND PICK IT UP, ALL THE DAY YOU'LL HAVE GOOD LUCK.

Solomon Grundy,
Born on
a Monday
Christened on Tuesday
Married on Wednesday
Took ill on Thursday
Worse on Friday
Died on Saturday
Buried on Sunday
This is the end of
SOLOMON
GRUNDY

Three blind mice! Three blind mice!
See how they run! See how they run!
They all ran after the farmer's wife.

Doctor Faustus was a good man,
He whipped his scholars now and then;
When he whipped them he made them dance

She cut off their tails with a carving knife.
Did you ever see such a sight in your life
As three blind mice?

Out of England into France,
Out of France into Spain,
And then he whipped them back again!

For want of a nail the shoe was lost,
For want of a shoe the horse was lost,
For want of a horse the rider was lost,
For want of a rider the battle was lost,
For want of a battle
The kingdom was lost,
And all for the want
Of a horseshoe nail.

THE MAN IN THE MOON LOOKED OUT OF THE MOON, AND THIS IS WHAT

Hey, diddle, diddle,
The cat and the fiddle,
The cow jumped over the moon;
The little dog laughed
To see such sport,
And the dish ran away with the spoon.

HE SAID, 'TIS TIME THAT, NOW I'M GETTING UP, ALL BABIES WENT TO BED.

There was an old woman
Tossed up in a basket,
Seventeen times as high as the moon.
Where she was going
I couldn't but ask it,
For under her arm she carried a broom.

Old woman, old woman, old woman, said I,
Where are you going to up so high?
To sweep the cobwebs out of the sky,
And I'll be with you by and by.

There was an old crow
Sat upon a clod;

That's the end of my song.
—That's odd.